Up in the Air

LEVEL 3

Written by: Marie Crook
Series Editor: Melanie Williams

Pearson Education Limited
Edinburgh Gate, Harlow,
Essex CM20 2JE, England
and Associated Companies throughout the world.

ISBN: 978-1-4082-8832-0

This edition first published by Pearson Education Ltd 2013
3 5 7 9 10 8 6 4
Text copyright © Pearson Education Ltd 2013

The moral rights of the author have been asserted
in accordance with the Copyright Designs and Patents Act 1988

Printed in Brazil by Docuprint DCPT 220206

Acknowledgements

The publisher would like to thank the following for their kind permission to reproduce their photographs:
(Key: b-bottom; c-centre; l-left; r-right; t-top)

Alamy Images: FotoCraft 6, 23 (a), David J. Green 13b, Image 17, INTERFOTO 20l, Luminis 1, NASA Archive 3l, 20r, 23 (c), Anthony Nettle 19, vario images GmbH & Co. KG 16t, A. T. Willett 12; **Corbis:** Steve Starr 13t; **Fotolia.com:** barefootpilot 3cl, 8, Gary 3r, 4-5, 23 (e); **Getty Images:** Scott Andrews 21, Vladimir Maravic 18, Joe McBride 7, Newsmakers / Tim Boyle 16bl; **Reuters:** Adrees Latif 15; **Shutterstock.com:** Dimon 14, 23 (b), Natali Glado 9, 23 (d); **SuperStock:** fStop 7 (inset), Tips Images 3cr, 10-11
Cover images: Front: **Fotolia.com:** Gary; Back: **Alamy Images:** Luminis

All other images © Pearson Education

In some instances we have been unable to trace the owners of copyright material,
and we would appreciate any information that would enable us to do so.

Illustration: Mark Ruffle

All rights reserved; no part of this publication may be reproduced, stored in a retrieval system,
or transmitted in any form or by any means, electronic, mechanical, photocopying,
recording or otherwise, without the prior written permission of the Publishers.

For a complete list of the titles available in the Pearson English Kids Readers series, please go to www.pearsonenglishkidsreaders.com. Alternatively, write to your local Pearson Education office or to Pearson English Readers Marketing Department, Pearson Education, Edinburgh Gate, Harlow, Essex CM20 2JE, England.

Contents

Small Aircraft — 4

Helicopters — 9

Jet Planes — 14

Rockets and Spaceships — 20

Activities — 23

Small Aircraft

Up in a hot air balloon! This is a fun way to fly!

The air gets hot and the balloon flies higher and higher.

The passengers look down. They see the people, trees and buildings get smaller and smaller.

A hot air balloon is an aircraft.

There are a lot of different kinds of aircraft. We use them for fun, for travel, for helping people and for learning.

Let's read more about different aircraft.

an **aircraft** flies in the air

hot air balloon

glider

runway

A glider is a small plane.

The glider does not have an engine. A propeller plane takes it into the sky. Then the glider uses the air.

Here the glider is taking off from the runway.

take off the aircraft leaves the runway

A hang glider is smaller than a glider. Only one pilot can fly this aircraft.

Many hang gliders take off from high places. The pilot moves his body and the aircraft moves round the sky.

hang glider

pilot

seaplane

Seaplanes can take off and land on water. We can fly seaplanes for fun.

Sometimes, when people have a problem at sea, seaplanes can help them. This seaplane is landing in the water.

land the aircraft leaves the sky and comes down again

Helicopters

Helicopters are very useful aircraft because they move in an interesting way.

When helicopters take off, they fly straight up into the sky. They do not have to use a runway. They can land in the same way.

helicopter

The rotor turns round and helps the helicopter fly. Helicopters can fly straight up, straight down and from left to right.

Helicopters can stop in the middle of the sky! They can do this because they have the rotor.

We can use helicopters many different ways. Because helicopters can take off and land in small spaces and stop in the middle of the sky, they can rescue people in mountains, forests and the sea. These can be dangerous places.

Firefighters often use helicopters in their work.

This is a forest fire. Here, the firefighters are putting water on the fire from the helicopter. Helicopters can carry a lot of water.

Helicopters can help television and radio stations. This helicopter is flying over a city and looking for problems or accidents on the roads below.

The television and radio stations can then tell people about any problems on the roads.

13

Jet Planes

This is an A380 jet plane. It has got four engines, 22 wheels and 16 passenger doors!

Jet planes fly higher and faster than many aircraft. They can carry many more people and they can travel very far.

jet plane a large aircraft for world travel

Many people travel by jet plane every day. This airport is very busy. Some people are travelling for work or holidays. Some people are visiting friends and family in different countries.

Jet planes can take us all round the world.

Here is the inside of a jet plane. You can find kitchens, televisions, beds and stairs on planes. These passengers are eating dinner.

Then, they can watch television or a film. They can listen to music or play computer games. And they can look out of the windows at the clouds!

The flight attendants work on the plane. They are very busy. They bring the passengers food and drink and help them with any problems.

cockpit

The pilot sits in the cockpit and flies the plane.

She talks to the passengers on the plane. She uses her radio. She tells them about the weather and the countries below. She can also talk to people in the airport. 'You can land now!' they say.

The pilot's job is very exciting. She flies all round the world and meets a lot of different people.

Rockets and Spaceships

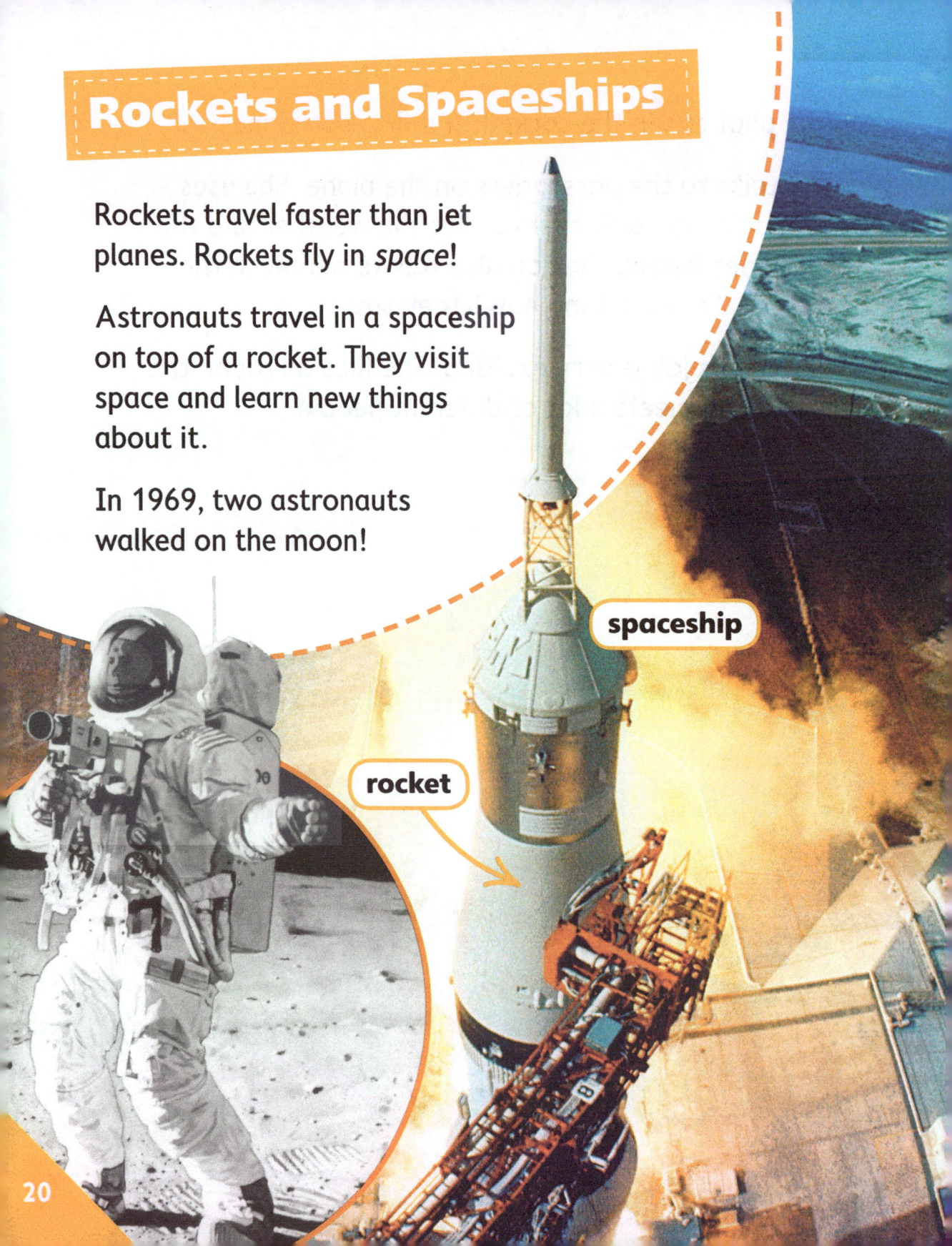

Rockets travel faster than jet planes. Rockets fly in *space*!

Astronauts travel in a spaceship on top of a rocket. They visit space and learn new things about it.

In 1969, two astronauts walked on the moon!

spaceship

rocket

space shuttle

This is a space shuttle. It has got a rocket and a plane. The rocket helps the space shuttle to take off and the plane helps it to land.

Space shuttles carry astronauts into space.

Would *you* like to travel in space? Perhaps one day you can!

We can now buy tickets for journeys into space. They are very expensive, but perhaps in ten years we can all travel to the moon for a holiday!

Activity page 1

Before You Read

1 **Match the words and pictures.**

> helicopter   jet plane   rocket   hot air balloon   glider

a   b   c

d   e

2 **Which of these can you find on a plane? Tick (✓).**

pilot ☐
balloon ☐
astronaut ☐
cockpit ☐
passenger ☐
airport ☐
flight attendant ☐

Activity page 2

After You Read

1 **Read and write Yes (Y) or No (N).**
   a   Helicopters have got propellers.
   b   A jet plane is slower than a glider.
   c   A glider has got an engine.
   d   We use hot air balloons for space travel.
   e   You can find a flight attendant on a jet plane.

2 **Answer the questions with a friend.**
   a   Can you say three aircraft?
   b   How does a hot air balloon fly?
   c   What does a pilot do?
   d   When do planes use a runway?
   e   What three things can you find on a jet plane?
   f   Why are helicopters useful?

3 Which is your favourite aircraft in the book?
   Why do you like it?
   Draw a picture of it. Tell your friend about it.